40 Whispers

for Couples

Slow the Pace of Your Life and Grow Your Intimacy.

JULIE GORMAN

Edited by Greg Gorman

40 Whispers Copyright © 2024 Greg & Julie Gorman

ISBN: 978-1-955546-75-1

All Scripture quotations are taken from the HOLY BIBLE, NEW INTERNATIONAL VERSION. ® Copyright © 1973, 1978, 1984 by Biblica. Used by permission of Biblica.

A Message from the Author

Hello Dear Friends,

In both the Old and New Testaments, the biblical theme of 40 days parallels with a season of preparation, testing, and time of transition for significant change. Moses fasted 40 days, 40 nights. Jesus draws away 40 days and 40 nights before entering his formal ministry time. The Father himself cleanses all creation with the flood, leading, sustaining, and keeping Noah and his family in an ark for 40 days and nights.

Over the next 40 days, I hope that you and your spouse transition your lives, marriage, and faith and experience significant renewal in hearing God's voice. May you encounter the power of a unified, intimate relationship with one another and the Father who still whispers to His children.

By His Grace and for His Glory,

Julie Gorman

Dedication

To my husband, best friend, and companion - Greg Gorman, you are the love of my life. Thank you for standing watch with me, always listening to and for His Gentle Whispers.

To my children, I pray you always hear His voice, encounter His presence throughout your life, and carry the blessing forward in your marriage and family.

And, most importantly, to my heavenly Father, You alone are my one pursuit. Thank You for loving me. Thank You for rescuing me. Thank You for speaking so gently to me, all the days of my life.

"Then, because so many people were coming and going that they did not even have a chance to eat, he said to them, "Come with me by yourselves to a quiet place and get some rest."

Mark 6:31

A Gentle Whisper

Day 1

Dear Son and Daughter, as you go through your day, remember I delight in you. I created you distinctly and set you apart for a purpose. Do not get distracted or discouraged. In moments of confusion or frustration, ask for my perspective and treat one another well. Throughout this day, look for opportunities to serve one another instead of expecting to be served. Your joy will return when you do your work as unto me. Do not do your acts of kindness expecting reciprocation, payback, or reward, but selflessly serve one another, preferring one another's needs over your own. Do your work as if you were serving me and refuse to keep score with one another. Let go of your offenses and love one another deeply. The world is looking to you and to your marriage.

Represent Me by demonstrating humility, unconditional love, and gentleness. You serve others so diligently; do not miss the beauty of serving within your home. Treat one another kindly. Offer encouragement to one another rather than complaints. Your love for one another reveals who I am to those who watch your relationship. Be gracious. Slow to anger. Abounding in love and good works. Be relentless in serving one another. And know this: I take joy when you lavish one another with love.

Gentle Whispers from God's Word

Colossians 3:23-24: "Whatever you do, work at it with all your heart, as working for the Lord, not for human masters, since you know that you will receive an inheritance from the Lord as a reward. It is the Lord Christ you are serving."

Philippians 2:1-4: "Therefore if you have any encouragement in Christ, if any comfort from His love, if any fellowship with the Spirit, if any affection and compassion, then make my joy complete by being like-minded, having the same love, being united in spirit and purpose. Do nothing out of selfish ambition or empty pride, but in humility, consider others more important than yourselves. Each of you should look not only to your own interests but also to the interests of others."

A Gentle Whisper Back

Father, help us to love as you have loved us unconditionally. Help us not to grow weary. Turn our hearts toward one another. Help us always to act graciously, tenderly, and affectionately as you intended for our relationship. In Jesus name, amen.

A Moment for Reflection

How did today's whisper challenge you? What one way can you better demonstrate humility and God's unconditional love?

Who does God say you are? Who does God say your spouse is? Take some time to listen for ways the Father wants to speak to your identity and encourage one another with His reminders.

Take a moment to ask and consider the following: what does God want for you? And what does He want from you?

A Gentle Whisper

Day 2

Son and Daughter, remember I created you for one another. Guard your heart and discipline your mind to look for what you love about one another, not what is lacking. As iron sharpens iron, I created you and your spouse distinctly to bring out the best in one another. Your differences are my design. Leverage them to grow yourself and strengthen one another. Do not resist or allow your differences to divide you. The enemy wants to deceive and frustrate you. Do not listen to his voice. He tells lies, trying to tear you apart. Refuse any message that you can't imagine me speaking. Instead, take every thought captive to who I say you are and who I say your spouse is; I will never speak death over you. Look and see your spouse as a human being who, like you, has needs, hurts, hopes, and dreams. But most of all, look and see they are mine. I fashioned them and entrusted you to nurture and bring out the best in them. I designed you perfectly, uniquely, just as I did your spouse. Be diligent in celebrating one another's design. Honor and demonstrate a mutual concern. And know this: I hand-crafted you and combined you together because two are better than one. And my plans for you are good and full of life.

Gentle Whispers from God's Word

1 Corinthians 12:18-25: "God has arranged the members of the body, every one of them, according to His design. If they were all one part, where would the body be? As it is, there are many parts, but one body. The eye cannot say to the hand, "I do not need you." Nor can the head say to the feet, "I do not need you." On the contrary, the parts of the body that seem to be weaker are indispensable, and the parts we consider less honorable, we treat with greater honor. And our unpresentable parts are treated with special modesty, whereas our presentable parts have no such need. But God has composed the body and has given greater honor to the parts that lacked it so that there should be no division in the body but that its members should have mutual concern for one another. If one part suffers, every part suffers with it; if one part is honored, every part rejoices with it."

A Gentle Whisper Back

Father, thank you for my spouse and for their gifts and talents. Help us always to honor what You have created. Help us to find what we love about one another, not what is lacking. Help us to always build on common ground and leverage our differences for your purposes. In Jesus' name, amen.

A Moment for Reflection

How did today's whisper challenge you? What one quality do you appreciate most about your spouse?

_____
_____
_____
_____
_____

Who does God say you are? Who does God say your spouse is? Take some time to listen for ways the Father wants to speak to your identity and encourage one another with His reminders.

_____
_____
_____
_____
_____
_____
_____

Take a moment to ask and consider the following: what does God want for you? And what does He want from you?

A Gentle Whisper

Day 3

Son and Daughter, why do you worry and doubt? Do you not know you can trust me? Do you not know I am for you? I will not betray your confidence. Though you face hardships, I will see you through. Remember the times I provided in the past. Remind yourself of my faithfulness and love. I am a loyal companion and friend. I will never leave you until I have fulfilled all that I promised you. I am God. There is no one like me. When I speak, none can refute. So, lean on one another and rest in me. I will lead you and sustain you. In your struggles, do not turn on one another. Instead, encourage one another and remind one another of what I have promised. When your heart grows weary, remember who I am and remind one another of who I say you are to me. Do not focus on the obstacles; look to me, and I will direct your steps and deliver you. Do not live limited by your abilities. Remember what I am capable of. Slow your pace together and meditate on my promises daily. I am faithful, and I will not disappoint you. Where two or three are gathered in unity and ask in accordance with my will, they will have what they ask for. Take hold of one another's hand and steadily call on me in prayer. I will listen. I will reply. Put your trust in me.

Gentle Whispers from God's Word

Matthew 18:19-20: "Again, truly I tell you that if two of you on earth agree about anything they ask for, it will be done for them by my Father in heaven. For where two or three gather in my name, there am I with them."

Philippians 4:6-7: "Do not be anxious about anything, but in every situation, by prayer and petition, with thanksgiving, present your requests to God. And the peace of God, which transcends all understanding, will guard your hearts and your minds in Christ Jesus."

A Gentle Whisper Back

Father, thank you for your reassuring words. Help us to release worry and doubt and fully trust in your faithfulness. We know you are for us and will see us through hardships. May we lean on one another and find rest in you. In moments of weariness, remind us of who we are. We come to you, hand in hand, trusting that you will listen and lead us in the way we should go. We put our trust in you. In Jesus name, amen.

A Moment for Reflection

How did today's whisper challenge you? How has God shown his faithfulness in your life, marriage, and family?

_____

_____

_____

_____

_____

_____

_____

Who does God say you are? Who does God say your spouse is? Take some time to listen for ways the Father wants to speak to your identity and encourage one another with His reminders.

_____

_____

_____

_____

_____

_____

_____

_____

Take a moment to ask and consider the following: what does God want for you? And what does He want from you?

A Gentle Whisper

Day 4

Son, Daughter, If this is all it is, will you serve me here? If your circumstances never change, will you remain faithful? Like David, when he stood before Goliath, will you recall my promises and fearlessly advance, trusting in my deliverance? Like Joshua and Caleb, will you believe me for the promised land, or will you cower before the giants? Your strength will grow when you turn your attention toward me rather than your circumstances. Steady your heart by steading your mind on the truth of who I am. Recall my kindness. Call on my power. I will never abandon you. Every moment of every day, I see you. When you feel as though you are alone, remind one another; I am near. Nothing can separate you from My love. I have not forgotten you. I see your struggles. I see your pain. I see how you tirelessly strive to do more and to be better. I see how you run from one activity to the next, hoping, wishing, and longing for fulfillment. Slow down. Draw near to Me, and I will draw near to you. I long to lift you up and give you strength. Today, listen to hear My voice; don't harden your heart toward Me or toward one another. Listen closely, and you will find what you need. Rest in Me, and you will find strength.

Gentle Whispers from God's Word

Psalm 139:7-10: "Where can I go from your Spirit? Where can I flee from your presence? If I go up to the heavens, you are there; if I make my bed in the depths, you are there. If I rise on the wings of the dawn, if I settle on the far side of the sea, even there your hand will guide me, your right hand will hold me fast."

Matthew 11:28-30: "Come to me, all you who are weary and burdened, and I will give you rest. Take my yoke upon you and learn from me, for I am gentle and humble in heart, and you will find rest for your souls. For my yoke is easy and my burden is light."

A Gentle Whisper Back

Father, we admit, at times, we've felt hurt, broken, and disillusioned. We want to surrender and not pick up any burdens again, but we need Your help. Intervene in our life and our marriage. Help us to rest in your presence and learn better how to hear you when you speak. Father, strengthen us. Restore our hearts and help our unbelief.

A Moment for Reflection

How did today's whisper challenge you? What is God asking you to believe for in this season of life?

_____

_____

_____

_____

_____

_____

_____

_____

Who does God say you are? Who does God say your spouse is? Take some time to listen for ways the Father wants to speak to your identity and encourage one another with His reminders.

_____

_____

_____

_____

_____

_____

_____

_____

Take a moment to ask and consider the following: what does God want for you? And what does He want from you?

A Gentle Whisper

Day 5

Son, Daughter, in this day, I am calling your words and heart into alignment. Speak in a manner worthy of being my child. Discipline your mind to meditate on whatever is true, noble, right, and pure. Even now, call into mind the things that caused you to fall in love with your spouse. Think about what you love about one another. Believe the best about each other. The familiarity of your marriage causes you to say things to one another that you would never dare say to another human being. But do not be mistaken; your words cut and damage your spouse like they would any other person. Your speech either brings life or death to your relationship, and none of them escape my notice. I hear every word. I see every deed. Live your life in a manner that brings me pleasure. Guard your words by guarding your heart, for out of the overflow of the heart, the mouth speaks. So, control your tongue by allowing Me to tame your heart. Be quick to release offenses and readily speak life and blessing over one another. Submit your thoughts, emotions, and speech to Me. I will help you control your words and help you to incline your hearts toward one another. Do not be rash with your words. Choose gentleness. Choose life. Remember, as you speak to one another, you are speaking to my child; honor and love them well.

Gentle Whispers from God's Word

Philippians 4:8: "Finally, brothers and sisters, whatever is true, whatever is noble, whatever is right, whatever is pure, whatever is lovely, whatever is admirable—if anything is excellent or praiseworthy—think about such things."

Proverbs 18:21: "The tongue has the power of life and death, and those who love it will eat its fruit."

A Gentle Whisper Back

Father, help us to meditate on what is good and pure about one another. Help us to speak life over one another and never harbor bitterness. Draw our hearts to you and toward one another. Thank you for our marriage. May all that we do and all that we say bring glory to you.

A Moment for Reflection

How did today's whisper challenge you? What quality do you most admire about your spouse?

_____

_____

_____

_____

_____

_____

Who does God say you are? Who does God say your spouse is? Take some time to listen for ways the Father wants to speak to your identity and encourage one another with His reminders.

_____

_____

_____

_____

_____

_____

_____

Take a moment to ask and consider the following: what does God want for you? And what does He want from you?

_____

_____

_____

_____

_____

A Gentle Whisper

Day 6

Son, Daughter, every moment of every day, I see you. I want to pour out my goodness and breathe life into your home. Will you participate with me? Will you do your part? Choose to follow me, to live for me, to do your work with integrity and excellence, even when no one else is watching. Choose to love without reservation. Don't put conditions on your humility. Choose to live in peace with one another. Soften your heart towards one another. Be sympathetic and compassionate. In all humility, do not repay evil with evil or insult with insult, but offer blessing and encouragement. Seek the interest of one another. Make it your desire to try to outdo one another in good works and lavish one another with acts of love. When you do, know this, you invite my presence and peace. Seek Me first and allow Me to fill you with My presence. I will refine your character to be more like Me, and in doing so, you will discover a life overflowing with every good thing. I give grace to the humble and increase the power of the weak. Strive to do what is good and pleasing in my sight and you will reap rich rewards. Forgive freely And love as I have loved you.

Gentle Whispers from God's Word

Colossians 3:13: "Bear with each other and forgive one another if any of you has a grievance against someone. Forgive as the Lord forgave you."

1 Thessalonians 5:15: "Make sure that nobody pays back wrong for wrong, but always strive to do what is good for each other and for everyone else."

A Gentle Whisper Back

Father, help us to be sympathetic and compassionate toward one another. We give you our thoughts and ask you to make us to be more like you. Provide for our needs and fill our home with joy, peace, and contentment.

A Moment for Reflection

How did today's whisper challenge you? What one way has God demonstrated his unconditional love to you?

Who does God say you are? Who does God say your spouse is? Take some time to listen for ways the Father wants to speak to your identity and encourage one another with His reminders.

_____

_____

_____

_____

_____

_____

Take a moment to ask and consider the following: what does God want for you? And what does He want from you?

_____

_____

_____

_____

_____

A Gentle Whisper

Day 7

Son, Daughter, trust in My love. When you feel weary, cast your cares on Me. Remember who I am. Remember who I have called you to be. Remember what I have promised you. I am the God who delivers. I am the God who parts the Red Sea. I am the God who shuts the mouths of lions. I am the God who promises not to withhold anything from the one who loves Me, who is called according to My purpose. Your impossibilities are possible to Me. So, what will you ask of Me? What do you need? Remember, I am good. My love for you endures forever. Just as you desire to give the best to those you love, so do I! Exchange your desires that are concerned with the temporal for what is eternal, and you will experience peace, joy, and contentment, whether in plenty or in need. The temporal constantly cries for your attention, so be diligent to pursue what is eternal. Daily, humble yourself in prayer, and I will show you a more excellent way to live. Strengthen your love for one another and surrender your plans, your agendas, and your concerns to Me. Entrust me with your spouse; entrust me with your relationship and family. Then watch and see what I will do. I hear your prayers. I care for your concerns. And I am able to do exceedingly above all you could ever ask, think, or imagine.

Gentle Whispers from God's Word

1 Peter 5:7: "Cast all your anxiety on him because he cares for you."

Psalm 34:17: "The righteous cry out, and the Lord hears them; he delivers them from all their troubles."

A Gentle Whisper Back

Father, at times, we feel weary, but You promised You would never leave us or forsake us. Empower us to surrender. Make our marriage better; Help us to be one another's best friends and live our lives to please you and live abundant, joy-filled lives. We release our agendas and timelines to you. Equip us to be the spouses You created us to be, and fulfill your call on our marriage.

A Moment for Reflection

How did today's whisper challenge you? If God were sitting with you today, and asked you: what one thing would you ask me for; what would you ask?

_____

_____

_____

_____

_____

_____

_____

Who does God say you are? Who does God say your spouse is? Take some time to listen for ways the Father wants to speak to your identity and encourage one another with His reminders.

_____

_____

_____

_____

_____

Take a moment to ask and consider the following: what does God want for you? And what does He want from you?

_____

_____

_____

_____

_____

A Gentle Whisper

Day 8

Son, Daughter, Listen closely and consider my words. Like a loving father, I am always looking out for you. I am working behind the scenes to pick you up and position you where I want when I want. Your delays are merely a preparation for your destiny. I am working behind the scenes to prepare your heart, refining you for my purposes. Will you serve me whether it's easy or not? Will you serve me whether anyone notices? Will you serve me in your family? I am using your relationship to refine your character to be selfless, full of hope, and abounding in mercy. Remember this: your marriage reveals your relationship with Me. How you treat one another reveals the clearest indication of your heart's condition. Humble yourself before Me and serve one another. Prefer one another's needs over your own. Remember, I will lead you. Serve and do your work as unto me, not whether you think one another deserves it but because you choose to serve and love one another as I have loved you. Surrender yourselves, independently, and then your desires as a couple to me. Remember, your complete surrender to Me is not a surrender that's reliant on your ability or reasoning or even in putting faith in yourselves or your spouse. Your surrender puts your hope and faith in Me alone. Don't worry. I won't let you down. Seek me daily, and I will meet with you and show you your part to walk in love, faithfulness, and forgiveness.

Gentle Whispers from God's Word

1 Corinthians 15:58 (NIV): "Therefore, my dear brothers and sisters, stand firm. Let nothing move you. Always give yourselves fully to the work of the Lord, because you know that your labor in the Lord is not in vain."

Ephesians 4:31-32: "Get rid of all bitterness, rage, and anger, brawling and slander, along with every form of malice. Be kind and compassionate to one another, forgiving each other, just as in Christ God forgave you."

A Gentle Whisper Back

Father, we confess how often we try to do things in our own power and live limited by what we can figure out. Lead us by your Holy Spirit, and we will follow. Be near to us. Let us sense Your direction and give us wisdom. Remind us of the promises contained in Your Word. Cause our marriage to thrive and be an earthly example of your unconditional love.

A Moment for Reflection

How did today's whisper challenge you? How is God asking you to serve him in this season of life?

Who does God say you are? Who does God say your spouse is? Take some time to listen for ways the Father wants to speak to your identity and encourage one another with His reminders.

Take a moment to ask and consider the following: what does God want for you? And what does He want from you?

_____
_____
_____
_____
_____
_____
_____
_____
_____
_____
_____
_____
_____
_____
_____
_____
_____

A Gentle Whisper

Day 9

Son, Daughter, I created you and your spouse to be one. I designed you to desire one another. To exclusively enjoy intimacy with one another inside your bedroom and to embrace life fully with one another outside of your bedroom. I designed you to enjoy sexual intimacy and oneness in marriage without shame. Do not live limited, and do not pervert what I created. Listen to My instruction and celebrate with one another fully. Do not resist one another; instead, enjoy one another's touch. Be satisfied with one another's bodies. Delight in one another and honor one another exclusively. Never share your love or affection with another. Act in a manner unworthy of my intent and design. Keep your marriage free from all unholiness. Protect what I have brought together. Don't let your marriage bed be defiled by the filth of this world. Let it be pure. Love one another with patience and kindness. Experience the complete freedom that I designed to be exclusively shared between a husband and wife. Love one another completely and without reservation. Do not deprive one another; instead, indulge in one another's love. Submit this sacred act to me, and let Me restore My intent in your relationship.

Gentle Whispers from God's Word

Proverbs 5:18-19: "May your fountain be blessed, and may you rejoice in the wife of your youth. A loving doe, a graceful deer—may her breasts satisfy you always, may you ever be intoxicated with her love."

Hebrews 13:4: "Marriage should be honored by all, and the marriage bed kept pure, for God will judge the adulterer and all the sexually immoral."

A Gentle Whisper Back

Father, You created sex exclusively for marriage. Fill our hearts with passion for one another and cause us always to desire one another exclusively as you intended. Grant us true freedom in this area of our marriage. Help us engage with one another sexually. We surrender this aspect of our marriage to You. Help us to be playful and to connect with one another completely. Help us know how to communicate freely about our desires and needs. And, if either of us holds a distorted view concerning sexual intimacy, convict us. Challenge our thinking and restore your intention and best for us. We submit our mind, body, and heart to You. Let us live free from the perversions of this world and one another as You intended, in Jesus' name, amen.

A Moment for Reflection

How did today's whisper challenge you? Is there any way you have lived limited to God's best in the bedroom? If so, consider what God desires for you in this most intimate aspect of marriage.

_____

_____

_____

_____

_____

Who does God say you are? Who does God say your spouse is? Take some time to listen for ways the Father wants to speak to your identity and encourage one another with His reminders.

_____

_____

_____

_____

Take a moment to ask and consider the following: what does God want for you? And what does He want from you?

A Gentle Whisper

Day 10

Son, Daughter, I never promised you a problem-free relationship, experiencing total bliss in every moment; I promised that I would be with you and provide you with comfort, counsel, and strength. In this day, look to serve instead of expecting to be served. Lean on one another's strengths instead of trying to change one another. I will provide you with wisdom, love, and direction. I will extend wisdom and the grace to accomplish the impossible, even when the seemingly impossible surrounds your marriage. Today, find what you love about one another, not what is lacking, and share how you appreciate love and respect one another. I am calling you to be light to this world. Let your relationship reflect my goodness, kindness, and love. Be strong and courageous. Do not be afraid or shrink back. Obstacles will not deter the inevitable. My promises for you are secure and will come to pass. Today, envision me at your side. Ask me for wisdom. Ask me for counsel. I will lead you in the way you should go. You don't have to do life on your own. I am with you and will never leave or abandon you. Remember my son's hands, his feet, his side. I did not reserve anything to rescue you. Remember the empty tomb. I defeated death and the grave. Time stands still at my command. Nothing is impossible to me. And know this: I am for you.

Gentle Whispers from God's Word

Joshua 1:9: "Have I not commanded you? Be strong and courageous. Do not be afraid; do not be discouraged, for the Lord your God will be with you wherever you go."

Matthew 20:26-28: Not so with you. Instead, whoerver want to become great myst be your servant and whoever want to be first must be your slave. Just as the son of

Man did not come to be served but to serve and give his life as a ransom for many.

A Gentle Whisper Back

Father, help us to walk in forgiveness. Remove any wrong attitudes that are causing us to become bitter or unkind to one another. Fill us with a greater desire to read your Word. And, as you promised. Help us to discern better your voice and your will for our marriage and family.

A Moment of Reflection

How did today's whisper challenge you? What one way will you take God at his word and fearless follow where he is leading?

_____

_____

_____

_____

_____

_____

Who does God say you are? Who does God say your spouse is? Take some time to listen for ways the Father wants to speak to your identity and encourage one another with His reminders.

_____

_____

_____

_____

_____

Take a moment to ask and consider the following: what does God want for you? And what does He want from you?

_____

_____

_____

_____

A Gentle Whisper

Day 11

Son, Daughter, Set aside time to pray specifically for one another and your marriage. As you pray, allow me to change in you the areas of your life that need to be changed. Don't focus on what one another needs to do better. Instead, ask me each day how I see you, how I see your spouse, and what I have to say about your life and marriage. Forgive where you need to forgive. Extend forgiveness even when it isn't sought after. Forgive as I forgave you. The world will tell you to take care of you. To hold on to your rights. To get even. But when you hold fast to bitterness and your rights, you bind them to your life and carry them as an ever-consuming poison in your body. Unforgiveness will steal your freedom and limit the joy I long for you to experience. Release your offenses and focus on how I want to grow you. There is so much I desire to reveal to you. Will you make time to listen? Instead of trying to do things on your own, will you ask for my help? I am faithful to answer when you ask me for anything in accordance with my will. Ask me to remove any wrong attitudes. Ask me to renew your love. Ask me to fill you with joy, peace, and abundant life. Then, sit back and watch me do exceedingly, abundantly more. Invite me to speak to you through My written word, and I will speak to you. I love you. I love your spouse. And I want to use your marriage as an earthly example of my love for the world.

Gentle Whispers from God's Word

Romans 12:2: "Do not conform to the pattern of this world, but be transformed by the renewing of your mind. Then you will be able to test and approve what God's will is—his good, pleasing, and perfect will."

John 13:34-35: "A new command I give you: Love one another. As I have loved you, so you must love one another. By this, everyone will know that you are my disciples if you love one another."

A Gentle Whisper Back

Father, help us to take responsibility for our own actions and not shift the blame to one another spouse. In every situation, show us how we can be pleasing to You. Equip us to bridle our thoughts and emotions and submit them to You. Help us to live according to Your Word.

A Moment for Reflection

How did today's whisper challenge you? What one way can you better demonstrate humility and God's unconditional forgiveness and love?

_____

_____

_____

_____

_____

_____

_____

Who does God say you are? Who does God say your spouse is? Take some time to listen for ways the Father wants to speak to your identity and encourage one another with His reminders.

_____

_____

_____

_____

_____

Take a moment to ask and consider the following: what does God want for you? And what does He want from you?

_____

A Gentle Whisper

Day 12

Son, Daughter, I have loved you with everlasting love. I am drawing you with loving-kindness. Listen closely for my direction. Seek me above all else. Be careful to protect your heart. Do not be distracted by the glitzy things of life; you cannot serve both God and money. So be careful of where you place your affection. Be alert; what you concentrate on will consume your attention and energy. There is a way that seems right to a man, but be on guard; the pursuit of riches corrupts. Money is not evil. It is a resource I want to entrust to you. Be undivided in your pursuit of me, and I will bless you as a resource to the nations. Be united in seeking me above all else, and everything else that you need will be provided. Don't be misled, Child. I long to give you good gifts. I long to lavish you with more, but I will not give you more than you can handle. I have granted you my favor; do not squander it on what will not satisfy—Steward what I have entrusted to you. Trust me as your provider. Everything you have has been granted by me. Entrust your abundance, entrust your needs, entrust desires to me alone. If you have any need, know this: you can trust me. Lift your voice together in unity; call on me, and I will answer.

Gentle Whispers from God's Word:

Matthew 6:24: "No one can serve two masters. Either you will hate the one and love the other, or you will be devoted to the one and despise the other. You cannot serve both God and money."

Proverbs 23:4-5: "Do not wear yourself out to get rich; do not trust your own cleverness. Cast but a glance at riches, and they are gone, for they will surely sprout wings and fly off to the sky like an eagle."

1 Peter 4:10: "Each of you should use whatever gift you have received to serve others, as faithful stewards of God's grace in its various forms."

A Gentle Whisper Back

Father, keep us from the love of money. We would never consciously choose money over you, yet at times we admit we do get sidetracked by the concerns of this world. So, help us to see you in our everyday lives. We trust for your provision. Help us to live generous lives. Everything we have is yours. Help us to steward all that you've entrusted to us in a manner worthy of your name.

A Moment for Reflection

How did today's whisper challenge you? Is there any earthly ambition distracting you from enjoying a more intimate relationship with God?

_____

_____

_____

_____

_____

Who does God say you are? Who does God say your spouse is? Take some time to listen for ways the Father wants to speak to your identity and encourage one another with His reminders.

_____

_____

_____

_____

_____

_____

Take a moment to ask and consider the following: what does God want for you? And what does He want from you?

A Gentle Whisper

Day 13

Son, Daughter, Sit quietly in My Presence and invite me to speak. Before you run headstrong, speaking and acting in your own power, pause and ask me for my thoughts. I will show you how to walk in unity and perfect love. Your unity multiplies your strength and power. Your differences are my design to bring about fullness and healing. I fashioned you to buffer one another and bring out the best in one another. Don't resist one another or look for one another's faults. The enemy wants you to hold on to offenses and turn one another down. Resist his lies and be careful not to resent one another's gifts. Leverage your differences. Celebrate them and learn from one another. Lean in and listen for my thoughts about your distinctions and how I want to use your lives for my glory.

You will grow and prosper as you build on common ground. Center your thoughts on who I am. Be humble, and I will lift you up and bring you joy beyond your greatest imagination. The strength of any team is in its diversity, which is why I brought you together. Meditate on your purpose and remember two are better than one because they have a good return for their labor and, when combined with my spirit, are undefeatable. I love you. I am for you. And, you honor me when you honor one another.

Gentle Whispers from God's Word

Psalm 133:1: "How good and pleasant it is when God's people live together in unity!"

Ecclesiastes 4:12: "Though one may be overpowered, two can defend themselves. A cord of three strands is not quickly broken."

A Gentle Whisper Back

Father, at times our tendency is to find fault with one another, but we know that isn't from You. Show us through Your Word and the power of Your Holy Spirit how to serve and love one another better. We submit our will to You and want to be pleasing in Your sight.

A Moment for Reflection

How did today's whisper challenge you? What attributes do you most love about one another?

_____

_____

_____

_____

_____

_____

Who does God say you are? Who does God say your spouse is? Take some time to listen for ways the Father wants to speak to your identity and encourage one another with His reminders.

_____

_____

_____

_____

_____

_____

Take a moment to ask and consider the following: what does God want for you? And what does He want from you?

_____

_____

_____

_____

A Gentle Whisper

Day 14

Son, Daughter, let my peace set your pace. Don't be consumed by the cares of this world. It makes vain promises that do not satisfy. So, don't be concerned by what you will accomplish or what you will attain; instead, slow your pace to stay in step with me. I will not disappoint you. I long for you to rid yourself of the could haves and should haves of life. Instead, be content to rest in my presence. Don't lie about your capacity. I never called you to do it all, nor do I expect you to. I called you to find contentment in Me alone. I designed and fashioned you to find joy in knowing me. Rid yourself of the busyness of life and allow me to lead you at a sustainable pace. Let worry, fear, and doubt drop from your shoulders. Envision me even now. Recall my power. Remind one another of who I am and that nothing is impossible with me. I am gentle of heart and strongly support those who are mine. Draw near to me, and I will draw near to you. Slow your pace and encourage one another. Remind one another that I am for you. Slow your pace and connect with Me, and the peace that surpasses all understanding will guard your heart and strengthen your soul.

Gentle Whispers from God's Word

Matthew 6:31-33: "So do not worry, saying, 'What shall we eat?' or 'What shall we drink?' or 'What shall we wear?' For the pagans run after all these things, and your heavenly Father knows that you need them. But seek first his kingdom and his righteousness, and all these things will be given to you as well."

Psalm 16:11: "You make known to me the path of life; you will fill me with joy in your presence, with eternal pleasures at your right hand."

A Gentle Whisper Back

Father, in the midst of the busyness and cares of this world, help us to slow our pace and align it with Yours. Teach us to find contentment in You alone and to let go of the could haves, should haves, and the desire for more. We surrender our worries, fears, and doubts at Your feet, trusting that You are in control.

A Moment for Reflection

How did today's whisper challenge you? Is there anything you need to let go of to better let his peace set your pace?

_____

_____

_____

_____

_____

_____

Who does God say you are? Who does God say your spouse is? Take some time to listen for ways the Father wants to speak to your identity and encourage one another with His reminders.

_____

_____

_____

_____

_____

Take a moment to ask and consider the following: what does God want for you? And what does He want from you?

_____

_____

_____

_____

_____

A Gentle Whisper

Day 15

Son, Daughter, Call out to Me and unify in prayer together. I have grafted you into My family, and your cries come before My very throne. You are safe with Me. Though you suffered for a little while, you will find hope and healing in My Presence. My perfect love casts out fear. So, remember, every trial, every offense, when yielded to Me, bears life. I will take what the enemy intended for evil and use it to reveal the depths and power of My love for you. You will walk through the fire and not be consumed. You will go through trials, but do not fear; I've granted you the power to overcome them. Be at peace and surrender your dreams, your desires, your hopes, and fears. Trust Me. Draw near to Me, and I will draw near to you. I hear the cries of my children. I answer prayers. I provide. I am unhindered and can do the impossible. Stir your faith by reflecting: who do you say I am? What you believe about me shapes how you live, and what you believe I think about you will impact every aspect of your life. Know this, son and daughter: I love you beyond measure and am attentive to your prayers. Let me be your hope, your resting place, your confidence, your victory. I will not ever abandon you, so never mistake my silence as my absence; I am ever present and working on your behalf.

Gentle Whispers from God's Word

Isaiah 41:10: "So do not fear, for I am with you; do not be dismayed, for I am your God. I will strengthen you and help you; I will uphold you with my righteous right hand."

Romans 8:28: "And we know that in all things God works for the good of those who love him, who have been called according to his purpose."

2 Corinthians 1:3-4: "Praise be to the God and Father of our Lord Jesus Christ, the Father of compassion and the God of all comfort, who comforts us in all our troubles so that we can comfort those in any trouble with the comfort we ourselves receive from God."

A Gentle Whisper Back

Father, we give you the permission to work in us and purify us. Remove every obstacle that hinders our walk with you or diminishes our intimacy with one another. Reveal any area we need to surrender to you and always help us walk in perfect peace, love and forgiveness.

A Moment for Reflection

How did today's whisper challenge you? Is there anything specifically God wants you to surrender and believe for His best in this season of life?

Who does God say you are? Who does God say your spouse is? Take some time to listen for ways the Father wants to speak to your identity and encourage one another with His reminders.

Take a moment to ask and consider the following: what does God want for you? And what does He want from you?

_____

_____

_____

_____

_____

_____

_____

_____

_____

_____

_____

_____

_____

_____

_____

_____

A Gentle Whisper

Day 16

Son, Daughter, Release your offenses so that you might know the joy of forgiveness and experience the hope found only in Me. Forgive as I forgave you. Accept one another, even as I have accepted you. Love one another, even as I have loved you. If you turn to Me, you will discover a love that removes the pain you once thought unbearable. The offenses that seemed unimaginable to forgive will vanish in light of the surpassing revelation of My love for you. I will create a new life in you, and you will be remade. When you extend forgiveness, you will more fully understand the depths of My love for you. And know this: I have loved you with an everlasting love. My love will sustain you and empower you to forgive. Be gentle with one another. You and your spouse are not the enemy. Look for and see the beauty of how I created you. Believe the best about one another. And then speak words of affirmation over one another, to one another. Soften your hearts. Let the gentleness of my spirit lead you. Be humble, and I will lift you up and restore joy and peace. Don't harbor shortcomings or rehearse messages of defeat; instead, practice praise and rehearse gratitude. My word will never fail. And, when you practice gratitude, you invite me to heal, deliver, and grant you a peace that surpasses all understanding. Son, daughter, you can trust me. You can trust in my love.

Gentle Whispers from God's Word

Luke 6:37: "Do not judge, and you will not be judged. Do not condemn, and you will not be condemned. Forgive, and you will be forgiven."

Proverbs 17:9: "Whoever would foster love covers over an offense, but whoever repeats the matter separates close friends."

Romans 15:7: "Accept one another, then, just as Christ accepted you, in order to bring praise to God."

Galatians 6:1: "Brothers and sisters, if someone is caught in a sin, you who live by the Spirit should restore that person gently. But watch yourselves, or you also may be tempted."

A Gentle Whisper Back

Father, we choose right now to release all the pain from our past. Help us to forgive and release offense. We want to be free from negative memories. We never want to harbor bitterness or anything that is not pleasing to You.

A Moment for Reflection

How did today's whisper challenge you? What one way can you better demonstrate humility and God's unconditional love?

Who does God say you are? Who does God say your spouse is? Take some time to listen for ways the Father wants to speak to your identity and encourage one another with His reminders.

Take a moment to ask and consider the following: what does God want for you? And what does He want from you?

A Gentle Whisper

Day 17

Son, Daughter, listen carefully to my leading. Hear my voice and do not shrink back. This is not a season to hold back. This is the season to dive deeper into My presence and listen intently for my voice. I will provide you with clear direction. Have I not promised that I will give wisdom to the one who asks? Do not try to figure it out on your own. Do not try to muscle through in your own power or strength. This is a day of intercession. This is the day to dive deep into your relationship with me and listen for all that I have in store. This is the day to hold fast to the promises I whispered to you concerning my plans and purpose for your life. Do not fall into despair. Do not give way to fatigue; instead, fall into my hands. Fall into my heart for you. Steady your heart and mind in the truth that you are dearly loved and are chosen by me. Therefore, I will push back the darkness and ferociously defend you. I will open the doors I want you to walk through. None will remain shut. But you must stand. You must follow my lead. You must defend your time with me, together. You must wait for my command. Do not shrink back. Do not shrink back. Do not shrink back!

Gentle Whispers from God's Word

Hebrews 10:39 (NIV) - "But we do not belong to those who shrink back and are destroyed, but to those who have faith and are saved."

1 Thessalonians 1:4 (NIV) - "For we know, brothers and sisters loved by God, that he has chosen you."

Revelation 3:8 (NIV) - "I know your deeds. See, I have placed before you an open door that no one can shut. I know that you have little strength, yet you have kept my word and have not denied my name."

A Gentle Whisper Back

Father, give us ears to hear Your wisdom and direction. Strengthen us to accomplish all You put before us. Thank You for every open door, and for closing doors that we wouldn't have the strength to close. We trust You and choose Your purposes and will over our own. Protect us, Lord, from those who would intentionally harm us or try to divide our marriage or family. Defend us. Help us to live in complete freedom and to love You and one another with all of our hearts. Show us how to demonstrate love and respect to one another. We release all of our "rights" and submit them to You. Help us to never shrink back, but to stand, and faithfully follow Your lead.

A Moment for Reflection

How did today's whisper challenge you? What one way can you stand firm in your faith, and advance forward to do what God has asked?

Who does God say you are? Who does God say your spouse is? Take some time to listen for ways the Father wants to speak to your identity and encourage one another with His reminders.

Take a moment to ask and consider the following: what does God want for you? And what does He want from you?

A Gentle Whisper

Day 18

Son, Daughter, Be quick to forgive an slow to become angry. Allow Me to infuse you with My love. The same grace that led you to Me will assist you in extending forgiveness. You are not alone! As you surrender your marriage to Me and forgive your spouse, I will heal your marriage. Forgive as God forgave you. Remember, no matter the offense, if you fail to forgive, you will miss the fullness I intended for you. Unforgiveness will cause you to suffer physically, emotionally, and spiritually. Instead, be compassionate. Let your spiritual eyes be opened to see how I see, understand what I know. Refuse accusation. There is only one place accusations derive. There is an accuser of the brethren. Do not align your thinking or your words to align with him. His way eads to death, pain, division. But, I have come that you might experience life. I AM the way, the truth, and the life. When you choose me, when you choose to resist what may seem counterintuitive, what may seem foreign to the way others tell you to respond, you will experience life, joy, peace, and the fullness of what I promise. Release everything to me. Let me be your defender. Let me heal what the enemy tried to destroy.

Gentle Whispers from God's Word

Ephesians 4:32: "Be kind and compassionate to one another, forgiving each other, just as in Christ God forgave you."

Matthew 6:14-15: "For if you forgive other people when they sin against you, your heavenly Father will also forgive you. But if you do not forgive others their sins, your Father will not forgive your sins."

A Gentle Whisper Back

Father, You said if we ask anything in accordance with Your will, You would hear us, and we would have whatever we asked for. So, thank You for helping us to forgive and to release every broken dream and painful memory. Erase every offense from our thoughts; help us never to ponder them again or use them as ammunition against one another. Make our marriage thrive, in Jesus' name. Amen

A Moment for Reflection

How did today's whisper challenge you? Is there anything that you need to release to better experience all God has for you?

_____

_____

_____

_____

Who does God say you are? Who does God say your spouse is? Take some time to listen for ways the Father wants to speak to your identity and encourage one another with His reminders.

Take a moment to ask and consider the following: what does God want for you? And what does He want from you?

A Gentle Whisper

Day 19

Son, Daughter, the friction you feel between one another at times is my process to reveal areas of your life that still need to be refined. Don't resist one another. Don't resist the learning process. Instead, lean in and I will free you from the things that hold you back from walking in perfect peace. As you surrender your attitudes and heart, you will find greater joy and life. I understand the process of removing those impurities can cause you pain, but trust Me, you will find freedom from its work. Quit looking at how your spouse needs to change. Entrust them to me. Allow me to change in them the things I see needing to be changed. And allow me to change in you the things that need to be changed. Quit wasting your time and exhausting your effort trying to do my job. I am the refiner. My Spirit sees clearly what needs to be purified. I will accomplish what you cannot. Will you trust me? Will you allow me to free you from the burden of control, fear, doubt, and anger? Will you rid yourself of the weight of trying to change another's heart? Your freedom comes in your personal surrender. Your freedom comes when you obey my lead. My commands provide your protection. I am a loving Father who sees perfectly, accurately, and without bias or limitation. You can trust me with everything; your dreams, desires, and life are safe with me. Listen for your part and entrust me to do mine. Entrust your spouse to me and love them, as I have loved you.

Gentle Whispers from God's Word

Malachi 3:3: "He will sit as a refiner and purifier of silver; he will purify the Levites and refine them like gold and silver. Then the Lord will have men who will bring offerings in righteousness."

2 Corinthians 3:18: "And we all, who with unveiled faces contemplate the Lord's glory, are being transformed into his image with ever-increasing glory, which comes from the Lord, who is the Spirit."

A Gentle Whisper Back

God, forgive us for entertaining any of the enemy's lies. we know Satan aims to destroy our marriage, so God, please help us to experience marriage as You intended. Heal and comfort our wounds. We commit our marriage to You. We long to know you more and to experience Your presence. Change us and help us to conform our desires to be like Yours. Each time we want to speak or think hateful thoughts, remind us of the love You hold for each of us. Remove our stubbornness, our pride, and our selfishness, and help us to forgive and love each other as You forgive and love us.

A Moment for Reflection

How did today's whisper challenge you? What one thing is God speaking specifically to you that you need to change? How is He asking you to grow?

_____

_____

_____

_____

_____

Who does God say you are? Who does God say your spouse is? Take some time to listen to ways the Father wants to speak to your identity and encourage one another with His reminders.

_____

_____

_____

Take a moment to ask and consider the following: what does God want for you? And what does He want from you?

A Gentle Whisper

Day 20

Son, Daughter, the spirit of this world shouts, Defend yourself. Take care of your needs. Get even. But listen closely, and I will teach you a more excellent way. Love your enemies. Pray for those who do you harm. Do good things for those who hate you or mistreat you. Forgive as I forgave you. Love as I have loved you. When you feel as though you have been misjudged, remember My love for you; remember how I never retaliated or paid back offense for an offense. Instead, I endured to bring about your salvation. My sacrifice brought your salvation. Your life is a precious gift that I long for you to enjoy. Don't waste it being offended. Don't squander your days by trying to get even. During this day, look for ways to speak life to one another, to your family, and to all I bring across your path. Be My love extended, and you will find great favor with Me and with others. See the beauty of all I created, both in nature and in others. Celebrate life. Meditate on what is good. Soak in all that surrounds your life. Look up. See the expanse of the sky. I stretched it wide with my word. Take notice of the gentle caress of the wind when it blows by. Don't miss the beauty of all my gifts. Your gratitude will free you from discontentment. Your thankfulness will invite my presence.

Gentle Whispers from God's Word

Matthew 5:44: "But I tell you, love your enemies and pray for those who persecute you."

Luke 6:27-28: "But to you who are listening I say: Love your enemies, do good to those who hate you, bless those who curse you, pray for those who mistreat you."

Romans 12:20-21: "If your enemy is hungry, feed him; if he is thirsty, give him something to drink. Do not be overcome by evil but overcome evil with good."

A Gentle Whisper Back

Father, You loved us so much that You sent Jesus to be the sacrifice for our sins and to restore us, by faith, to a right relationship with you. We know that sins separate us from experiencing you more. Help us to forgive freely and love one another in action. Help us always to speak life and be gentle in our responses. Help us to love one another and others. We are so grateful for Your Holy Spirit and Your grace. Help us to love with all of our hearts, as You have loved us.

A Moment for Reflection

How did today's whisper challenge you? What one thing are you most grateful for? What do you love most about your spouse?

_____

_____

_____

Who does God say you are? Who does God say your spouse is? Take some time to listen for ways the Father wants to speak to your identity and encourage one another with His reminders.

Take a moment to ask and consider the following: what does God want for you? And what does He want from you?

A Gentle Whisper

Day 21

Son, Daughter, in the beginning, I spoke and all that is, came into being. I pushed back darkness with just the mention of light, and I set into motion all that exists. Likewise, the power of life and death are in the tongue. When you speak, you set into motion my law of sowing and reaping. If you sow words of healing, kindness, and life, you will reap hope, compassion, and blessing. If you sow contentious words, words filled with hate and strife, expect the same. So, guard your words well by guarding the thoughts you entertain. Refuse accusation. Refuse to align your thoughts with the enemy of your soul. He is the accuser of the brethren and wants you to believe lies about you, your spouse, your family, and all my creation. Do not give an ear to his voice. The 'you'll nevers' and the 'you should get evens' are not my voice. My voice is redemptive, not condemning. My voice is encouraging, not derogatory. My voice is certain, not confused. I am not uncertain. I am specific and clear. My voice brings peace, not fear. Spend time with me. Study my character. Look for me in every moment of every day. And remember this: You are not alone. I will never leave you abandoned. I will rise to your cause and defend you. Bare My character and demonstrate My love, and you will witness My deliverance. Align your thinking with mine and refuse any messages that contradict Who I am or who I say you and your spouse are to me. One day, you will give an account of both your words and deeds. Humble yourself now. Take responsibility for your actions and confess your sins so that you might be healed and experience the fullness of my love and good intent for your life.

Gentle Whispers from God's Word

James 5:16: "Therefore confess your sins to each other

and pray for each other so that you may be healed. The prayer of a righteous person is powerful and effective."

Ephesians 4:29: "Do not let any unwholesome talk come out of your mouths, but only what is helpful for building others up according to their needs, that it may benefit those who listen."

A Gentle Whispers back

Father, You promised to give wisdom to all who ask. We ask You for wisdom. Give us discernment so we can avoid falling prey to the enemy's lies. We desire to love one another as you intended. Help us to guard our words by guarding our thoughts and intention of our hearts. Help us always to be kind-hearted, compassionate, and slow to anger. We acknowledge love is not just an emotion but a choice and an action. Help us walk out Your unconditional love with a sincere heart. Make our marriage thrive and be an example that provides hope for others, in Jesus' name. Amen.

A Moment for Reflection

How did today's whisper challenge you? What one characteristic do you most appreciate about your spouse? Your kids? Your life? How can you better welcome God's words of life over your life?

_____

_____

_____

_____

_____

Who does God say you are? Who does God say your spouse is? Take some time to listen for ways the Father wants to speak to your identity and encourage one another with His reminders.

_____

_____

_____

Take a moment to ask and consider the following: what does God want for you? And what does He want from you?

A Gentle Whisper

Day 22

Son, Daughter, Seek me above all things. Riches, fame, selfish ambition will only leave you longing for more. Contentment resides in my presence. Gratitude welcomes my favor. Guard the ambition of your heart. Your desires set into motion inescapable consequences. Seek me. Pursue me with all your heart. Don't lean on your own ingenuities or wisdom. Instead make every effort to seek a greater revelation of Who I Am and how much I love you and you will find peace, joy, and great contentment. I will rescue you and give grace in your time of needs. Reside in My peace. Slow your pace. Create time to actively listen for my lead. Only I can satisfy the true longings of your soul. Center your life and marriage in me by asking Me each day: Father, show us how to love our family and one another in such a way that will cause all of us to experience You more. Change our hearts to walk in humility and defer to You in all things. When you do, you will receive grace and peace. You will walk with a new lightness to your step. Anxiety will flee. Fear will fade. Hope will restore.

Gentle Whispers from God's Word

Matthew 6:33: "But seek first his kingdom and his righteousness, and all these things will be given to you as well."

James 4:6: "But he gives us more grace. That is why Scripture says: 'God opposes the proud but shows favor to the humble.'"

Psalm 37:7: "Be still before the Lord and wait patiently for him; do not fret when people succeed in their ways, when they carry out their wicked schemes."

Colossians 3:15: "Let the peace of Christ rule in your hearts, since as members of one body you were called to peace. And be thankful."

A Gentle Whisper Back

Father, help us to walk in humility. Cause us to see the world not only through our eyes, but also through Your eyes, and the eyes of one another. Help us humble our own desires and offer compassion toward each other and understand what we each think and feel. Help us resolve our conflicts and reach a middle ground of understanding with one another. Knit us together as one. Help us create new habits and develop a family structure founded on Your Word. Grant us the ability to leave a legacy of love for our children.

A Moment for Reflection

How did today's whisper challenge you? Is there anything

distracting you or weighing on your heart that God wants you to surrender to Him?

_____

_____

_____

_____

_____

Who does God say you are? Who does God say your spouse is? Take some time to listen for ways the Father wants to speak to your identity and encourage one another with His reminders.

_____

_____

_____

_____

_____

Take a moment to ask and consider the following: what does God want for you? And what does He want from you?

A Gentle Whisper

Day 23

Son, Daughter, Hear Me. Do not lie about your capacity. I never designed you to do it all. I never called you to do it all. Listen to My warning. Be on guard; your enemy seeks to destroy and entice you away by your desires. He masks himself as an angel of light, but his "wisdom" is steeped in lies filled with selfish gain. His ways seem right, but in the end produce death. Commit your ways to Me and experience true satisfaction and joy. Follow the example of My Son. He drew away to find rest. He only did what He saw me do. He only spoke what He heard Me speak. Submit your life, your marriage, your family to Me. Choose to follow my lead. Seek Me with all of your heart that you might know the truth and live in the fullness I provide. I will put a new heart in you, one that craves after Me and rejoices in the truth. I will captivate you with my goodness and grant you true wisdom. Delight in Me and experience the fullness of the love and joy I intended for your life. What you really believe about me will overshadow everything you do. What you believe that I believe about you, will shape your entire life. Today, challenge your thoughts. Decide what you really believe about me and listen closely to what I speak about you. I have loved you with an everlasting love. I am drawing you with loving-kindness. Everything I speak, is for your good. Every command is given for your well-being. Will you trust me? Will you surrender to my plan? Will you listen to my voice and obey my Word? Draw near to me child, and I will draw near to you.

Gentle Whispers from God's Word

Ephesians 6:11: "Put on the full armor of God so that you can take your stand against the devil's schemes."

James 4:7: "Submit yourselves, then, to God. Resist the devil, and he will flee from you."

1 Peter 5:8: "Be alert and of sober mind. Your enemy the devil prowls around like a roaring lion looking for someone to devour."

A Gentle Whisper Back

Father, forgive us for being judgmental. Help us to be all You ask and live out the purpose You designed for our marriage. We give You every thought, feeling, and emotion. Create in us a pure heart. Cause us to walk righteously and live with a loving, gentle spirit. Make our marriage thrive. May our own desires and agendas never cloud the path that You desire for our marriage. We yield to Your will for us. We surrender our expectations in exchange for Your sovereign will. Make our marriage thrive we pray in Jesus' name. Amen.

A Moment for Reflection

How did today's whisper challenge you? What one way can you better demonstrate humility and God's unconditional love?

_____

_____

_____

_____

_____

Who does God say you are? Who does God say your spouse is? Take some time to listen for ways the Father wants to speak to your identity and encourage one another with His reminders.

_____

_____

_____

_____

Take a moment to ask and consider the following: what does God want for you? And what does He want from you?

A Gentle Whisper

Day 24

Son, Daughter, Focus your attention on Me, the Giver of Life. I will sustain you. I will uphold you by My righteous right hand. I will offer life to you and breathe hope into your marriage and family. I am your starting point and your point of reference. When you feel discouraged, remember I am near. When you feel abandoned, remember you are not alone. When you feel you can't take another step, I will carry you. When you don't know which way to turn, I will instruct you. I truly am with you. What seems impossible to you and too big to overcome is not too difficult for Me. I know what you need; nothing is hidden from My sight. Lean into Me and I will grant you wisdom. Ask me and I will give you strength. Remember who I am and remind yourself of my love, and fear will fade. From everlasting to everlasting, I am. I do not change. My character and love stand true. I will deliver you. I will uphold you. You have nothing to fear. Cast your worries far from you. Dance. Sing. Laugh. Walk free from doubt and fear; they have NO part of you. Your future is secure, for I am faithful, and I am your God. I blot out your sins and say you are free. Walk with confidence, trusting that I will do all I have promised. Doubt only your doubt. And remember WHO I AM. My mercy is neverending and my strength knows no end.

Gentle Whispers from God's Word

Psalm 46:1: "God is our refuge and strength, an ever-present help in trouble."

Psalm 32:8: "I will instruct you and teach you in the way you should go; I will counsel you with my loving eye on you."

A Gentle Whisper Back

Father, indeed, Your Spirit is active and alive! We invite You to move on our marriage. Restore any intimacy the enemy has stolen from us. Strengthen us when we feel weak. Defend us in our time of trials. Teach us how to die daily to our own selfish desires and surrender our marriage to You more fully. We want all that you have for us. Grant us wisdom and strength, and deliver us from all evil, in Jesus' name, amen.

A Moment for Reflection

How did today's whisper challenge you? What one way can you better demonstrate humility and God's unconditional love?

_____

_____

_____

_____

Who does God say you are? Who does God say your spouse is? Take some time to listen for ways the Father wants to speak to your identity and encourage one another with His reminders.

Take a moment to ask and consider the following: what does God want for you? And what does He want from you?

A Gentle Whisper

Day 25

Son, Daughter, Lean in and listen for my lead. Listen intently, and you will hear me. Look for me in all things. Search for me with all your heart. Do not let your heart be troubled. I have loved you with everlasting love. I have drawn you in loving kindness. I always fulfill my promises. My intention for your life will be established. And all that I have planned for you will come to pass. I have ordained your steps and will make your paths straight. You wonder what you should do; you worry about so many things. Instead of worrying, discipline your mind to focus on and rest in me. Remember who I am. Remember my faithfulness. Reflect on my goodness. Even when you are faithless, I remain faithful. I see you, child, and I have not forgotten you. Join your hearts together. Grab one another by the hand and worship me together. For where two or three are gathered, I am in the midst. I am attentive to your cries. I will send My Spirit to guide you and fill you. He will counsel you and show you how to live. Commit your way to Me, and I will grant you the joy and peace of My presence. I will do this for My name's sake and because I love you. Recommit to prayer. Meditate on my promises. Allow me to renew the desires of your heart and bring peace to your life and marriage.

Gentle Whispers from God's Word

Psalm 37:5-6: "Commit your way to the Lord; trust in him, and he will do this: He will make your righteous reward shine like the dawn, your vindication like the noonday sun."

John 14:26: "But the Advocate, the Holy Spirit, whom the Father will send in my name, will teach you all things and will remind you of everything I have said to you."

Romans 15:13: "May the God of hope fill you with all joy and peace as you trust in him, so that you may overflow with hope by the power of the Holy Spirit."

A Gentle Whisper Back

Father, we commit our ways, our ideas, and our desires to you. We pray as you told us to pray; your kingdom come; your will be done in our lives, on this earth, as it is in heaven. We put our trust and confidence in you. You are the same God who worked miracles in the past. Lead us. Fill us with your presence. Help us to walk in the confidence of who we are in you, your children.

A Moment for Reflection

How did today's whisper challenge you? What one way can you better demonstrate humility and God's unconditional love?

Who does God say you are? Who does God say your spouse is? Take some time to listen for ways the Father wants to speak to your identity and encourage one another with His reminders.

Take a moment to ask and consider the following: what does God want for you? And what does He want from you?

A Gentle Whisper

Day 26

Son, Daughter, I delight in your obedience. I rejoice over your faithfulness. My plans are to fill you with the fullness of My life and the joy that comes in knowing Me. In this world, you will be tempted and tested. But each time you choose to listen and obey, each time you take up your cross to follow Me, you will receive from Me what can never be taken away—the joy of My salvation—the security of My faithfulness—the joy of My love! Be quick to listen and slow to become angry. Do not harbor grudges or fill your mind with accusations toward one another. Instead, be merciful even as I have been merciful to you. Let the meditations of your heart be on what you love about one another. Partner with me by speaking life and encouraging one another.

Refuse offense. Refuse accusations. Refuse fear, jealousy, or any dissension. Instead, take authority over your mind and your actions daily. Do not be overwhelmed by evil but overcome evil by doing good. Remember, my spirit lives in you. You hold power and authority to walk in step with him. So, do not be overwhelmed. I am with you. I will strengthen you, shield you, and protect you. Love one another without reservation; do your acts as unto me; in doing so you honor me.

Gentle Whispers from God's Word

Psalm 37:4 (NIV): "Take delight in the Lord, and he will give you the desires of your heart."

Zephaniah 3:17 (NIV): "The Lord your God is with you, the Mighty Warrior who saves. He will take great delight in you; in his love, he will no longer rebuke you, but will rejoice over you with singing."

Romans 12:21 (NIV): ""Do not be overcome by evil but overcome evil with good."

A Gentle Whisper Back

You alone are God. You alone judge righteously without fault; remind us to never to judge one another. Convict us of any sins causing divisions between us. May we never shift the blame to one another, but in humility, cause us to serve one another. Give us the wisdom to resist the devil's lies. And help us to forget any disparaging words we've spoken over one another. Soften our hearts and tame our tongues. Help us to establish checkpoints that keep us from quarreling and better help us keep you at the center of our home.

A Moment for Reflection

How did today's whisper challenge you? What one way can you better demonstrate humility and God's unconditional love?

_____

_____

Who does God say you are? Who does God say your spouse is? Take some time to listen for ways the Father wants to speak to your identity and encourage one another with His reminders.

Take a moment to ask and consider the following: what does God want for you? And what does He want from you?

Gentle Whisper

Day 27

Son, Daughter, Will you trust Me? Will you follow after Me? Will you love as I have loved you? Allow me to empower you with My Spirit. Seek Me, that you might find life and hope for your soul. Don't demand your way; be humble, and I will grant you grace. Be gentle and patiently serve one another. Make every effort to live according to My Spirit. For in My Spirit, there is fullness of life. Seek peace and pursue it, and My ears will be attentive to your prayers. In this day, what would you ask me for? What do you desire? I long to do exceedingly above all you can ask, think, or imagine. Remove every weight that entangles you from following after me. The world says to defend, fight for your rights, and take care of what you need. Instead of demanding your way or trying to change or control one another, be humble and kind. Have I not said what I love? Do you not remember what I require? But to act justly. Love mercy. And, walk humbly. Entrust one another to my care. Share your concerns with me. Give me the thoughts that consume your days. I will provide. I will protect you. I will uplift you. And, I will deliver you. When you slow your pace and seek me, I will not disappoint you. My Spirit will grant you love, joy, peace, and gentleness. Do not lean on your own understanding or rely on your own abilities; instead, submit every thought and feeling to me and I will grant you strength to walk with goodness, kindness, and the power to do what is right.

Gentle Whispers from God's Word

1 John 4:11-12 (NIV): "Dear friends, since God so loved us, we also ought to love one another. No one has ever seen God; but if we love one another, God lives in us and his love is made complete in us."

Galatians 5:22-23 (NIV): "But the fruit of the Spirit is love, joy, peace, forbearance, kindness, goodness, faithfulness, gentleness and self-control. Against such things there is no law."

Gentle Whispers Back

Father, thank you for your Spirit. Thank you for your peace. Thank you that you hear our prayers and care for every one of our concers. Help us never to turn on one another but to always temper our words by the power of your Holy Spirit. Lead us and direct our steps. And may all that we do and all that we say bring glory to you.

A Moment for Reflection

How did today's whisper challenge you? What one way can you better demonstrate humility and God's unconditional love?

_____

_____

_____

_____

_____

What ministered to me from God's whisper today?

_____

_____

_____

_____

_____

Who does God say you are? Who does God say your spouse is? Take some time to listen for ways the Father wants to speak to your identity and encourage one another with His reminders.

_____

_____

_____

Take a moment to ask and consider the following: what does God want for you? And what does He want from you?

Gentle Whisper

Day 28

Son, Daughter, Be careful not to follow after worldly wisdom; bring your thoughts in line with Mine. Consider and follow My ways, and you will not be ashamed. Remember My commands and be faithful to do them; then you will be blessed. Though the world instructs you to declare your rights, I have provided you with a better example to follow. Serve as I served you. Resist self-promotion, pride, or ungratefulness. Don't be unforgiving, conceited, or lovers of pleasure; rather, be a lover of Me. Indeed, there will be ways that seem right to you, but in the end, they produce death. My words bring life and produce a joy unspeakable, full of my glory. Follow Me in order that you might live. Keep my promises before you, and do not turn from them. Be steady and know that I will do all that I have promised. When you love like I loved you, you invite me to work miracles on your behalf. When you unconditionally love one another, you experience even more fully my presence in your life. When you persevere together, you experience the joy and unity that can only be experienced by enduring adversity and making it through to the other side. But be encouraged. I will not leave you to do this on your own. Call on me, and I will help you. Draw near to me and at every turn ask me for wisdom. I will direct you and show you how to love and live in unity with one another.

Gentle Whispers from God's Word

Proverbs 3:5-7 (NIV): "Trust in the Lord with all your heart and lean not on your own understanding; in all your ways submit to him, and he will make your paths straight. Do not be wise in your own eyes; fear the Lord and shun evil."

Deuteronomy 6:6-7 (NIV): "These commandments that I give you today are to be on your hearts. Impress them on your children. Talk about them when you sit at home and when you walk along the road, when you lie down and when you get up."

A Gentle Whisper Back

Father, make our love new. Give us the ability to serve one another in love. Help us enjoy one another fully. Let us grow together instead of apart. Help us to renew our commitment daily and to be sensitive to one another's needs. Let spontaneity flow in our relationship. Assist us to support one another unselfishly. Alleviate any tension building between us. Let Your peace reign in our marriage and a life-giving atmosphere in our home. Don't allow anything to hinder us from communicating life to one another, and help us not to be so serious. Instead, help us to live light-heartedly and find joy and contentment together. In Jesus' name. Amen!

A Moment for Reflection

How did today's whisper challenge you? What one way has God demonstrated His love to you that He is asking you to demonstrate to your spouse or family?

_____

_____

_____

_____

_____

Who does God say you are? Who does God say your spouse is? Take some time to listen for ways the Father wants to speak to your identity and encourage one another with His reminders.

_____

_____

_____

_____

Take a moment to ask and consider the following: what does God want for you? And what does He want from you?

Gentle Whisper

Day 29

Son, Daughter, Listen to Me. Quiet the noise and remove the busyness and distractions. of your life. Instead, spend some time with Me. Allow me to remind you of the truth of who you are and of what is most important. In this life you will be tested and face many trials, but I will send My Spirit to you to assist you. As you draw near to Me, you will experience true love, joy, and peace. You will gain greater patience. I will equip you with kindness. As you surrender afresh your heart's desires and release your emotions, feelings, and thoughts, I will help you govern your speech. Let your heart be filled with love for Me, and you will discover treasures far greater than worldly riches. Think of the most beautiful scenery you've ever encountered, and remember this: I created it. If I can create such majesty if I can govern the stars and tell the moon and sun when and where to rise, is my arm too short to care for your every concern? Your relationship, your family, your job, your home, I see everything, and I will never abandon you. I've got you, child. I will hold your children. I've secured your legacy. Refuse worldly wisdom. Refuse fear. Only doubt your doubts, for they are not from me. I will lead you with assurance and confidence. Trust me, and peace will be your friend. Follow my lead, and you will never be disappointed. When you have questions, ask. When you have concerns, share them with me. And, always extend love to one another, and you will experience a glimpse of my unconditional love through one another.

Gentle Whispers from God's Word

Psalm 46:10 (NIV): "He says, 'Be still, and know that I am God; I will be exalted among the nations, I will be exalted in the earth.'"

Colossians 3:12 (NIV): "Therefore, as God's chosen people, holy and dearly loved, clothe yourselves with compassion, kindness, humility, gentleness, and patience."

Gentle Whispers Back

Father, so many things weigh on our hearts. We long to experience you more fully. We long to hear your voice. Please speak in such a way that we don't miss you or confuse your thoughts with any other. Today, we want to renew our minds and experience the fullness of your spirit in our lives and marriage. We put our trust in you. Thank you for the beauty that surrounds us every day. Help us to catch glimpses of you throughout our day. Help us to walk humbly, do justice, and extend mercy and love to one another and others you bring across our path, in Jesus' name we pray. Amen.

A Moment for Reflection

How did today's whisper challenge you? Take a moment to envision the place that brings you the most peace. See it clearly in your mind. Imagine, God created that beauty and wanted to share it with you. How does that kind of love inspire you?

_____

_____

_____

_____

_____

Who does God say you are? Who does God say your spouse is? Take some time to listen for ways the Father wants to speak to your identity and encourage one another with His reminders.

_____

_____

_____

_____

_____

_____

Take a moment to ask and consider the following: what does God want for you? And what does He want from you?

Gentle Whisper

Day 30

Son, Daughter, listen carefully to my instruction; be slow to become angry. Pay careful attention to the thoughts you think. A man will reap what he sows. If you entertain how you are always the one who has to sacrifice, and always having to be the one who puts forth the effort, you will be sure to find more supporting evidence for those thoughts. Eventually, you will convince yourself those thoughts are true, and you won't be able to see anything else. But, if you look for what is good and try to catch one another doing what is right, you will discover a whole new narrative that will connect you with one another and produce greater intimacy and friendship. Doesn't my word command you to think on what is good, pure, and of a noble report? Children, learn from Me. Seek me. I will turn your brashness to gentleness. The things that once controlled you, you will overcome. I will teach you how to demonstrate self-control in your relationships. Offenses will fall to the wayside as you meditate on who I am and follow after who I have called you to be. I will teach you to love what is good and to resist what is evil. Entrust your life and your marriage to Me. I will not disappoint you; you will taste My goodness and bear the fruit of My Spirit. Even now, breathe in. Breathe out. Let your heart find comfort in knowing I am near. Slow your thoughts. Meditate on what is good. Throughout this day, let my peace set your pace and govern your words and actions toward one another.

Gentle Whispers from God's Word

James 1:19-20 (NIV): "My dear brothers and sisters, take note of this: Everyone should be quick to listen, slow to speak and slow to become angry, because human anger does not produce the righteousness that God desires."

Deuteronomy 7:9 (NIV): "Know therefore that the Lord your God is God; he is the faithful God, keeping his covenant of love to a thousand generations of those who love him and keep his commandments."

Gentle Whispers Back

Father, at times, we know we push our way, plead our case, and insist that one another listen to our needs. Help us to follow your command to think about what is good so that the overflow of our hearts speaks words of comfort and love. Cause us to focus on one another's good qualities and not belabor negative thoughts. Guard our mouths and help us to build one another up, not tear one another down, in Jesus' name. Amen.

A Moment for Reflection

How did today's whisper challenge you? What one way can you better demonstrate humility and God's unconditional love?

_____

_____

_____

_____

_____

Who does God say you are? Who does God say your spouse is? Take some time to listen for ways the Father wants to speak to your identity and encourage one another with His reminders.

_____

_____

_____

_____

Take a moment to ask and consider the following: what does God want for you? And what does He want from you?

Gentle Whisper

Day 31

Son, Daughter, pursue one another and love one another without reservation. Don't withhold anything good from one another. If an expectation from one another aligns with what is good and doesn't misalign with my word, choose to serve and honor one another and meet one another's needs. Soften your heart don't be easily offended. Instead, be gentle, humble, kind, and compassionate with one another. I designed your relationship to reflect my love. Think and consider; how I have loved you. Think and consider; do your actions and words bring me honor? Love and serve one another, as unto me. Be affectionate and kindhearted, and deal gently with one another, in word and deed. Know this: This is the one I esteem; he who is humble in spirit and contrite in heart. Look for ways to demonstrate my love. Extend kindness and grace. It brings me pleasure when you love one another as I have loved you. Look for ways to demonstrate love to one another like you did when you first fell in love. Treat one another kindly, treasuring one another as I intended. Practice tenderness. Extend compassion. Be sensitive to one another's needs, attentive, and affectionate toward one another. It brings me pleasure when you look to serve one another.

Gentle Whispers from God's Word

Proverbs 19:11 (NIV): "A person's wisdom yields patience; it is to one's glory to overlook an offense."

1 John 4:7-8 (NIV): "Dear friends, let us love one another, for love comes from God. Everyone who loves has been born of God and knows God. Whoever does not love does not know God, because God is love."

Gentle Whispers Back

Father, help us to walk humbly and to demonstrate love. Cause us to remember and believe the best about one another. Fill our days with new life and laughter. And Father, help us to care for one another, serve one another, and always be kind toward one another as you have commanded.

A Moment for Reflection

How did today's whisper challenge you? Take a moment to reflect and consider: What one way can you better serve your spouse? What one thing have they asked you to do that you could do today?

_____

_____

_____

_____

_____

Who does God say you are? Who does God say your spouse is? Take time to listen for ways the Father wants to speak to your identity and encourage one another with His reminders.

_____

_____

_____

_____

_____

Take a moment to ask and consider the following: what does God want for you? And what does He want from you?

_____

_____

_____

_____

_____

_____

Gentle Whisper

Day 32

Son, Daughter, Slow down. Breathe. Rest in Me. Every day, many things grab your attention. Quit striving and remember what is most important. The fool runs after his own wisdom. The arrogant make plans in their heart and never give thought to Me. But you were destined for so much more. I never designed you for misery. I want to clothe you with My strength and cover you with My peace. Choose what is better. Love as I have loved you. Serve with all humility, for I esteem the humble of heart. Who do you desire to impress? Who will you serve—yourself or Me? By choosing what is better, you will taste what is best and will know the joy found only in Me. I will lead you. When you feel like demanding your way, choose to refuse selfishness. When you feel like giving up or grow tired of doing good, ask Me, and I will give you strength to stand firm. I will renew your strength and steady your heart. When you feel hurt, betrayed, or disappointed, surrender to Me in prayer, and I will strongly support you! Whoever loses his life for My name's sake will find it. Humility is foolishness to this world, but you will never go wrong by listening to my wisdom and choosing to follow my lead.

Gentle Whispers from God's Word

Isaiah 40:29 (NIV): "He gives strength to the weary and increases the power of the weak."

Matthew 16:25 (NIV): "For whoever wants to save their life will lose it, but whoever loses their life for me will find it."

Gentle Whispers Back

Father, help us to walk in unity in our faith and unwaveringly follow you. Incline our hearts toward you and also toward one another. Help us to reject worldly wisdom that tries to get us to declare our rights and instead follow you, serving one another with gentleness and humility, in Jesus' name, amen.

A Moment for Reflection

How did today's whisper challenge you? What one way can you better demonstrate humility and extend God's unconditional love?

_____

_____

_____

_____

_____

Who does God say you are? Who does God say your spouse is? Take some time to listen for ways the Father wants to speak to your identity and encourage one another with His reminders.

Take a moment to ask and consider the following: what does God want for you? And what does He want from you?

Gentle Whisper

Day 33

Son, Daughter, do not be hasty with your words or take for granted the gift I've entrusted to you. Your spouse is my child. I made them in my image and crafted you for one another. Be infatuated, smitten, and enraptured with their design. Explore and discover the depths of their being both in and outside of the marriage bed. Protect your heart by carefully protecting what you entertain. Keep your eyes free of temptation by living fascinated with your spouse. Do not be lured by the world's distortion of sex. They pervert what I ordained. Delight in one another. Ask me my intent. Ask me what my best is for your intimacy. Then, be diligent to never settle for anything less than My best. Rid your fears of inadequacy by focusing on your spouse, not your shortcomings, and your desire for one another will grow. Do not disdain what I have called good, holy, and pure. Seek me in this area, and I will heal every part of what the enemy has attempted to destroy.

Gentle Whispers from God's Word

Proverbs 4:23 (NIV): "Above all else, guard your heart, for everything you do flows from it."

Song of Solomon 4:7 (NIV): "You are altogether beautiful, my darling; there is no flaw in you."

Genesis 2:23-24 (NIV): "The man said, 'This is now bone of my bones and flesh of my flesh; she shall be called 'woman,' for she was taken out of man.' That is why a man leaves his father and mother and is united to his wife, and they become one flesh."

Gentle Whispers Back

Father, keep us free from temptations. Don't let us ever be enticed or lured toward this world's distortion of sex. Cause us to find one another exciting, intoxicating, and appealing. Rid us of any fears of inadequacy—and any doubts about our design. Help us to fulfill one another's desire and ejnyo the safety of an exclusive oneness with one another. We invite You to be the God of our marriage bed and to help us experience Your best in our intimacy, in Jesus' name. Amen!

A Moment for Reflection

How did today's whisper challenge you? Today, consider this thought: How can you protect your marriage bed and better honor your spouse?

_____

_____

_____

_____

_____

_____

Who does God say you are? Who does God say your spouse is? Take some time to listen for ways the Father wants to speak to your identity and encourage one another with His reminders.

_____

_____

_____

_____

_____

Take a moment to ask and consider the following: what does God want for you? And what does He want from you?

_____

_____

_____

_____

_____

_____

Gentle Whisper

Day 34

Son, Daughter, Do you feel disconnected? Do you feel alone? Remember, you reap what you sow. Take time to plant the right seeds and safeguard your relationship. Don't take one another for granted. Instead, live intentionally to stay connected. Take time to grow together. Seek every opportunity to add value to one another. Rather than complaining, feeling hurt, or shifting blame, take time to connect, renew your love, and rediscover the reasons why you married. Be loyal, devoted, and committed to paying close attention to one another. Grow your friendship by building on what you share. Dream together. Laugh together. Catch one another doing what is good and right. Determine to spend time in my presence worshiping, praying, and seeking me. I will defend you and protect you and cause my spirit to unite you in perfect peace. Steady your heart by centering your mind on me. I have granted you access to my favor. My favor will expand further and farther than your greatest imagination. In moments of doubt and in moments of confusion, simply ask: Father, who do you say we are, and what do you have to say about our circumstances? And know this, son and daughter ... YOU are mine. At just the right time ... I will do the extraordinary and the exceptional. Your unity is powerful. When you unite in prayer, choose to align your faith, and ask me for anything that aligns with my will, know this: you will receive what you ask for. I will not withhold any good thing to those who ask.

Gentle Whispers from God's Word

Ephesians 5:33 (NIV): "However, each one of you also must love his wife as he loves himself, and the wife must respect her husband."

Proverbs 3:3-4 (NIV): "Let love and faithfulness never leave you; bind them around your neck, write them on the tablet of your heart. Then you will win favor and a good name in the sight of God and man."

Isaiah 26:3 (NIV): "You will keep in perfect peace those whose minds are steadfast because they trust in you."

Gentle Whispers Back

Father, help us to stay connected intentionally. Help us always to love and treasure one another. Life gets so busy, and we have so many responsibilities. Help us to protect what matters most. Encourage our hearts and strengthen our love, in Jesus's name, amen.

A Moment for Reflection

How did today's whisper challenge you? What one thing do you believe God wants to intervene on your behalf? How can you better pursue Him and unite in prayer about your concerns?

_____

_____

_____

_____

_____

Who does God say you are? Who does God say your spouse is? Take some time to listen for ways the Father wants to speak to your identity and encourage one another with His reminders.

_____

_____

_____

_____

_____

Take a moment to ask and consider the following: what does God want for you? And what does He want from you?

Gentle Whisper

Day 35

Son, Daughter, Know this: I am able to do immeasurably more than you could ever ask, think, or imagine. If you ask Me for anything in accordance with My will, I will hear you and give whatever you ask in My name. Fix your thoughts on Me. Ambition ruins many people. They run after things that will never satisfy them. Guard your heart. Pursue me, and I will give you everything you need. I will fulfill all I've promised you. But I won't give it all at once, lest your promise overtake and overpower you. Because you love Me, I will protect you. I will not give you more than you can handle. Trust Me. Don't make plans in your own wisdom; instead, listen intently to My instructions. Don't weary yourself by trying to accomplish things in your own power; instead, follow closely and walk in steps of obedience. I have loved you with everlasting love. My heart delights in you. I listen to you when you pray. I delight in your love. My eye is ever upon you. So, take heart. I will defend you. I will strongly support you as you put your trust in me. Abandon your timelines, seek me above all others, and intently search for me, listening for my voice. I will speak and whisper my thoughts to you. Like two friends, let's talk together and share our secrets. I will share with you what is yet to come and listen as you share what concerns you. And know this, as you wait, as you listen, as you engage and grow in your love for me, you will find everything that you need in this life. You are not alone. I will move on your behalf.

Gentle Whispers from God's Word

Ephesians 3:20 (NIV): "Now to him who is able to do immeasurably more than all we ask or imagine, according to his power that is at work within us."

1 John 5:14 (NIV): "This is the confidence we have in approaching God: that if we ask anything according to his will, he hears us."

Isaiah 30:21 (NIV): "Whether you turn to the right or to the left, your ears will hear a voice behind you, saying, 'This is the way; walk in it.'"

Gentle Whispers Back

Father, we desire to be all You want us to be. Teach us how to encourage one another. Let the words of mouth be ones of blessings, not curses. Grant us wisdom to promote Your perfect will and plan for one another. Cause us to see one another's strengths and express verbal praise over one another daily. Help us to be best friends and always support one another's dreams, in Jesus' name, amen.

A Moment for Reflection

How did today's whisper challenge you? What is one way you can support and encourage your spouse as you both wait for Him to answer your prayers? Is there something you can do? Is there something you can say? If you are open to one another and don't feel defensive, ask your spouse how you can better encourage and support them.

_____

_____

_____

_____

_____

Who does God say you are? Who does God say your spouse is? Take some time to listen for ways the Father wants to speak to your identity and encourage one another with His reminders.

Take a moment to ask and consider the following: what does God want for you? And what does He want from you?

Gentle Whisper

Day 36

Son, Daughter, let my peace set your pace. Cease striving and find the joy of resting in my presence. The Sabbath was intended for you to find rest from your work. Choose a day to set aside to replenish your soul. Quit focusing on your capabilities. Confidence in yourself will never lead you where I am taking you. Instead, keep your face resolute on me and seek me together. Faith comes by hearing, but you will miss my voice if you do not slow your pace. Self-ambition leaves a weight that I never intended you to carry; exchange it for my passion. When you feel as if you can't breathe or begin to get consumed by the what ifs or if only's of life, slow down so that you can catch up with me. Let me give you a Heaven-to-Earth vision instead of the Earth-to-Heaven vision that leaves you feeling overwhelmed. Make it your mission to know me, love me, and follow me together in unity. I have loved you with an everlasting love, even now I am working things together for you as you daily surrender your will for mine. Center your life and decisions on me. Listen for my wisdom. Despite the hardships of this world…Despite the evil plots of men. You need NOT fear because I AM GOD! When I speak, no one can refute it. I whispered the world into existence and breathed life into man. Steady your heart by centering your mind on me. I have granted you access to my favor. My favor will expand further and farther than your greatest imagination. In moments of doubt and in moments of confusion, simply ask: Father, who do you say I am, and what do you have to say about this? And know this child… YOU are mine. At just the right time … I will do the extraordinary and accomplish the exceptional.

Gentle Whispers from God's Word

James 1:5 (NIV): "If any of you lacks wisdom, you should ask God, who gives generously to all without finding fault, and it will be given to you."

Romans 12:1-2 (NIV): "Therefore, I urge you, brothers and sisters, in view of God's mercy, to offer your bodies as a living sacrifice, holy and pleasing to God—this is your true and proper worship. Do not conform to the pattern of this world, but be transformed by the renewing of your mind. Then you will be able to test and approve what God's will is—his good, pleasing and perfect will."

Gentle Whispers Back

Father, we know at times we pick things up and run ahead of you, and then get frustrated when things don't go as we have planned. Today, we surrender once again to your perfect will and plan. Lead us. Direct us. And help us to walk in step with you. Help us to love one another well and seek you in unity together.

A Moment for Reflection

How did today's whisper challenge you? What one way can you better demonstrate humility and God's unconditional love?

_____

_____

_____

_____

_____

Who does God say you are? Who does God say your spouse is? Take some time to listen for ways the Father wants to speak to your identity and encourage one another with His reminders.

Take a moment to ask and consider the following: what does God want for you? And what does He want from you?

Gentle Whisper

Day 37

Son, Daughter, breathe. Listen. Wait for my direction. Hear my voice. Remember my love. You did not choose me, but I chose you and appointed you that you would bear much fruit. Seek me, and you will find rest for your soul. The world shouts for you to do, for you to accomplish, for you to strive. I long for you to laugh and take joy in your life journey. Your life was meant to be enjoyed, not conquered. Contentment comes by seeking me above all else. Then, whether you are in plenty or in want, you will find peace. Quiet confidence will be your friend because you hear and know my plans, and rest knowing I will do what I say. You will not add one minute or one accomplishment more than what has been granted. Let me take the lead. Let me lift your weights. I comfort all who mourn. I am close to the broken-hearted and save those who are crushed in spirit. Today, lean into one another. Hold one another's hands and ask me to intervene where you have need. I strongly support those who are mine and faithfully deliver my children from the paths of destruction. Encourage one another with these words. My Spirit will equip you, empower you, and encourage you. My Spirit searches all across the land to strongly support the ones who are completely mine. So, breathe, child, breathe. I have not abandoned you. The assignment I've called you to is not a burden for you to solve or a mission of sacrifice; rather, it is a gift for you to treasure. I AM your partner. I am your security. I am your resource.

Gentle Whispers from God's Word

John 15:16 (NIV): "You did not choose me, but I chose you and appointed you so that you might go and bear fruit—fruit that will last—and so that whatever you ask in my name the Father will give you."

Philippians 4:12-13 (NIV): "I know what it is to be in need, and I know what it is to have plenty. I have learned the secret of being content in any and every situation, whether well fed or hungry, whether living in plenty or in want. I can do all this through him who gives me strength."

Psalm 34:18 (NIV): "The Lord is close to the brokenhearted and saves those who are crushed in spirit."

A Gentle Whisper Back

Father, comfort us and encourage us. Lead us in the way we should go and grant us the peace that surpasses all understanding. Thank you that you are faithful. We put our trust in you. Help us to experience the contentment you shared and remind us quickly of your goodness if we get discouraged. In Jesus' name, amen.

A Moment for Reflection

How did today's whisper challenge you? What one way can you better let God take the lead? Is there anything you need to release to him that you've picked up? Share together any concerns that you can pray about together.

_____

_____

_____

_____

_____

Who does God say you are? Who does God say your spouse is? Take some time to listen for ways the Father wants to speak to your identity and encourage one another with His reminders.

_____

_____

Take a moment to ask and consider the following: what does God want for you? And what does He want from you?

Gentle Whisper

Day 38

Son, Daughter, do you see me? Do you see what I'm up to? Delight in me, and I will grant you the desires of your heart. Your gratitude and celebration of praise release me to do the impossible. It is my pleasure to give good gifts to those I can trust. When you look at what you don't have, you only crave more. Your desires leave you wanting and longing for the things that never satisfy. But, when you carry a heart of gratefulness, even if you are in want, you will experience contentment and the joy of knowing me more. You find what you are looking for, so be sure to look for what is worthy of praise. Search for what is good. Let the meditations of your heart be to offer me thanks. I inhabit your praises and extend goodness and mercy to all who call on me. Do you desire to give good gifts? Do you take joy when those you love appreciate what you've done for them? So do I. Know this Son and Daughter, I am a rewarder of those who diligently seek after me. I am not limited by your lack, nor am I deterred by your struggles. Ask me and I will show you a more excellent way to live. A life free from the weights of this world. A place where you will live unmoved by the circumstances of life. I am unshakable. And those who rest in my presence will be protected and secure. Throughout this day, practice gratitude and remember who I am. Though you have suffered for a little while I will redeem you and deliver you from the fire. Make me your dwelling place and no harm will prosper against you. Meditate on my promises and remember I am faithful to fulfill the words of my messengers. You will see the glory of my works, for I take pleasure in you. You are my joy and my delight.

Gentle Whispers from God's Word

Psalm 91:1-2 (NIV): "Whoever dwells in the shelter of the Most High will rest in the shadow of the Almighty. I will say of the Lord, 'He is my refuge and my fortress, my God, in whom I trust.'"

Matthew 7:7-8 (NIV): "Ask and it will be given to you; seek and you will find; knock and the door will be opened to you. For everyone who asks receives; the one who seeks finds; and to the one who knocks, the door will be opened."

Gentle Whispers Back

Father, so many things call for our attention and try to intimidate our faith. But, we choose you. You are worthy of our trust. We take you at our word to be our defender, protector, and provider. Thank you for hearing our prayers and providing for our needs. Grant us wisdom, direction, and your incredible favor in every area of our life, marriage, and family. In Jesus' name, amen.

A Moment for Reflection

How did today's whisper challenge you? Take a moment to consider and share your responses with one another: What one thing are you most grateful for about your spouse? What one thing are you most grateful for that God has given you?

_____

_____

_____

_____

_____

Who does God say you are? Who does God say your spouse is? Take some time to listen for ways the Father wants to speak to your identity and encourage one another with His reminders.

_____

_____

_____

Take a moment to ask and consider the following: what does God want for you? And what does He want from you?

Gentle Whisper

Day 39

Son, Daughter, submit to one another and give one another respect. Remember, you are my children, act accordingly. When you are angry, do not treat one another unkindly. Instead, choose to extend forgiveness and grace and be patient with one another. If you are weary and feel like you are at an impasse, instead of trying to figure it out on your own, seek me together. Fill your heart and your home with praise for me, and I will soften your hearts and show you how to move together and build on unity. Ask yourselves and consider what I have to say about your circumstances. Do not harden your hearts or draw harsh lines in the sand. Consider how one another is right and build on peace, truth, gentleness, and life. Do not let your emotions carry you away or listen to the accuser of the brethren. He likes to twist and misconstrue your identity. He lies and tries to convince you that you are right and superior. My voice never condemns. My words are full of life and hope. Call on me, and I will help you. Refuse to entertain any messages that do not convey my love, and you will find peace in your soul. It may seem counterintuitive. It may feel like you are being a doormat. But love is humble, kind, not easily angered, and always perseveres. You hold the power to choose to forgive. Your forgiveness is not a doormat. Your choice to release offense and forgive freely models after my son, who, though he was wrongfully treated, prayed; Father, forgive them for they know not what they do. That kind of selfless love invites unconditional love and will soften even the most heated arguments.

Gentle Whispers from God's Word

James 3:17: "But the wisdom that comes from heaven is first of all pure; then peace-loving, considerate, submissive, full of mercy and good fruit, impartial and sincere."

Ephesians 5:21: *"Submit to one another out of reverence for Christ."*

Gentle Whispers Back

Father, help us to always extend unconditional love and respect to one another, mutually submitting to one another out of our reverence to you. Help us to be slow to become angry, quick to listen, and abounding in love for you and for one another. In Jesus' name, amen.

A Moment for Reflection

How did today's whisper challenge you? What one way can you better express life to your spouse and demonstrate Christ's humility and unconditional love?

_____

_____

_____

_____

_____

_____

Who does God say you are? Who does God say your spouse is? Take some time to listen for ways the Father wants to speak to your identity and encourage one another with His reminders.

_____

_____

_____

_____

_____

_____

Take a moment to ask and consider the following: what does God want for you? And what does He want from you?

Gentle Whisper

Day 40

Son, Daughter, Your marriage demands your constant effort to die to yourself and pursue a life of giving, not taking. If you find yourself growing resentful, keeping score, or becoming impatient, slow down. Remember, every journey has a starting point; your marriage started with a vow before Me to love, honor, and cherish one another. Look for every opportunity to live that practically. Recommit intentionally discover ways to put your spouse's needs before your own. Then, watch me move! Ask of me, and I will restore your love, joy, and peace. Consider who I am and remember what I am capable of. Think of this: who parted the Red Sea? Moses? No, but Moses witnessed My faithfulness and felt the limitlessness of My power when he obediently outstretched his hand toward it. My purpose will be accomplished. My plans for your life and marriage will be fulfilled. Don't worry about what your spouse needs to do. You only need to rest and watch My deliverance, being careful to do all I have called you to do. Don't worry. Don't fear. My plans for you and your spouse are good, and My mercy endures forever. I will turn your hearts toward one another; your part is to do YOUR part.

A Gentle Whisper from God's Word

Psalm 27:14 (NIV): "Wait for the Lord; be strong and take heart and wait for the Lord."

Isaiah 30:18 (NIV): "Yet the Lord longs to be gracious to you; therefore, he will rise up to show you compassion. For the Lord is a God of justice. Blessed are all who wait for him!"

Micah 7:7 (NIV): "But as for me, I watch in hope for the Lord, I wait for God my Savior; my God will hear me."

A Gentle Whisper Back

Father, help us always to see the best and believe the best about one another. Help us not to grow weary in doing good and serving one another. Help us to find ways to renew our love and honor our vows daily. Increase our love for one another, and may our hearts always to true to our first love with you and always see the best name, amen.

A Moment for Reflection

How did today's whisper challenge you? What one way can you better demonstrate humility and God's unconditional love?

_____

_____

_____

_____

_____

Who does God say you are? Who does God say your spouse is? Take some time to listen for ways the Father wants to speak to your identity and encourage one another with His reminders.

_____
_____
_____
_____
_____
_____

Take a moment to ask and consider the following: what does God want for you? And what does He want from you?

_____
_____
_____
_____
_____
_____
_____

www.ingramcontent.com/pod-product-compliance
Lightning Source LLC
Chambersburg PA
CBHW050859160426
43194CB00011B/2219